DOGGY
KNITS

DOGGY
KNITS

10 ORIGINAL
PATTERNS FOR YOUR
STYLE-CONSCIOUS
DOG

Alison Jenkins

Dover Publications, Inc.
Mineola, New York

Bibliographical Note:
Wacky Doggy Knits, first published by Dover Publications, Inc. in
2014 is an unabridged republication of the edition published by Ivy
Press Limited, Lewes, United Kingdom in 2007.

Manufactured in the United States by Courier Corporation
78012001   2014
www.doverpublications.com

Library of Congress Cataloging-in-Publication Data

Jenkens, Alison.
Wacky doggy knits: 10 original patterns for your style-conscious dog /
Alison Jenkens.
     pages cm
ISBN 978-0-486-78012-2 (alk. paper)
1. Knitting—Patterns. 2. Dogs—Equipment and supplies. I. Title.

TT825.J4283 2014
746.43'2—dc23

2013039875

ISBN-13: 978-0-486-78012-2
ISBN-10: 0-486-78012-0

Printed in China

This book was conceived, designed, and produced by
Ivy Press
210 High Street, Lewes,
East Sussex BN7 2NS, U.K.

Creative Director Peter Bridgewater
Publisher Jason Hook
Editorial Director Caroline Earle
Art Director Sarah Howerd
Senior Project Editor Mary Todd
Senior Designer Suzie Johanson
Designer Clare Barber
Photography Andrew Perris Photography
Publishing Assistant Anna Stevens

Picture Credits iStockphoto: Atwag: 33 left; Albert Campbell: 39;
Pavel Lebedinsky: 33 top right, 35 top; Lisa Thornberg: 35 right.

ACKNOWLEDGMENTS
Many thanks to all the owners and their fabulous dogs:

Salty Sea Dog and Buzzy Bee: Tracy Potter and Egg and Chips
French Couture: Christine Reynolds and Jake
Superhero and Sunflower: Angela Chadwick and Roxy and Polly
Bellboy: Sophie Collins and Ted
Eskimo Chic: Sue Warde and Sumo
Preppy Sweater: Andrew Lawes and Ellie
Giddy Up: Sandra Hurst Chico and Bertie
Froggy Fashion: Lesley Harvey with Buffy

CONTENTS

iNTRoDUCTioN

PERSONALITY, STYLE, POISE, CHARM, GOOD LOOKS—you've either got them or you haven't. Ask a hundred dog owners to describe their canine companion and you'll be sure to get a hundred very different replies. Every dog is an individual, with his or her own character traits and funny little habits—just like human beings!

To create individual examples of canine couture for stylish dogs, *Doggy Knits* contains ten unique outfits for man's (and woman's) best friend, so cute that you won't be able to resist digging out your knitting needles and getting started. Each outfit in this book can be hand-knitted to fit your dog perfectly. Knitted fabric is by nature soft, flexible, and extremely comfortable—what could be better for the dog in your life?

If you've never knitted before, don't worry—it won't be a problem. The first section of this book shows you exactly how to knit, with clear step-by-step instructions, from the very first cast-on stitch right through to the bind off. A whole range of knitting stitches and techniques are covered, including the knit stitch, purl stitch, stocking stitch, rib combinations, Fair Isle patterns and borders, and fabulous Intarsia color work.

In fact, you'll have all the information you need to easily complete any of the outfits in the book—hats and accessories included. All the patterns have been designed with the beginner in mind, so they are simple to knit and construct for a great-looking result. The knitting-up instructions are given in clear explanatory text with charts and helpful diagrams, while making-up details and any decorative effects are shown with step-by-step photographs and instructions.

Throughout the book you will also find lots of hints, tips, tricks, and shortcuts to make the knitted variety of canine couture a breeze. So, take a long, hard look at your pooch and decide what would suit him or her best—the crisp salty sea dog look or a fluffy buzzy bee sweater? Maybe a smart French-style jacket and beret, or a colorful jockey shirt would be the best choice to fit your furry friend's personality to a T?

Knitting is a compulsive hobby—even more so when you can share it with your pet. All the dogs in this book enjoyed modeling the knits—and your doggy will be sure to enjoy wearing the results of your knitting endeavors every bit as much.

How could I fail to get an A plus in my doggy obedience exam today?

BASIC EQUIPMENT

The hand knitter requires very little equipment to get started—needles, yarn, and a bodkin will usually suffice for most patterns! See below for other bits and pieces that will prove useful for your doggy knitting projects.

NEEDLES

* Knitting needles can be made from plastic, metal, wood, or bamboo. They have a blunt point at one end and a knob at the other to prevent the stitches from falling off.
* Double-ended needles come in sets of four or five and are used for knitting in the round. Circular needles can also be used for this purpose and are usually sold in pairs in a choice of sizes.
* Cable needles are short, double-ended needles used for holding stitches when working cables or twists.

NEEDLE CHART

When you buy yarn the suggested needle size is printed on the label—although it's best to knit a sample first to check the tension (see page 13).

US	METRIC
0	2 mm
1	2.25 mm
2	2.5 mm
3	3 mm
4	3.5 mm
5	3.75 mm
6	4 mm
7	4.5 mm
8	5 mm
9	5.5 mm
10	6 mm
10 1/2	6.5, 7, 7.5 mm
11	8 mm
13	9 mm
15	10 mm
17	12.75 mm
19	16 mm
35	19 mm

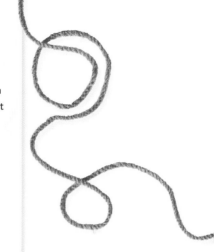

OTHER EQUIPMENT

✳ BODKIN—a needle with a large eye and a blunt point, used for sewing knitted pieces together and for decorative work.

✳ SMALL SCISSORS—keep a pair of small, sharp embroidery scissors to hand for snipping off yarn.

✳ STITCH HOLDER—this is rather like a giant safety pin! It is handy for holding stitches that are not in use when working necklines and other shapings.

✳ RULER—a plastic ruler is more useful than a cloth or plastic measuring tape for checking tension swatches.

✳ PINS—buy pins with large glass or plastic heads so you won't lose them in your knitting. Use them for marking out tension swatches and pinning garment pieces together.

✳ ROW COUNTER—although not absolutely necessary, this is useful. A little plastic device, it is slipped onto the end of the needle to help you keep an accurate row count.

✳ TAPE MEASURE—used for taking measurements.

YARN

Yarns fall broadly into four categories: light weight, medium weight, heavy weight, and bulky. See below for stitch yield per 4 in (10 cm) sample, and suggested needle sizes.

✳ LIGHT WEIGHT—available in 2, 3, 4, and 5 ply, these yarns are generally used for baby and children's garments. Stitch yield: 25–32. Needle size: 1–4 (2.25–3.5 mm).

✳ MEDIUM WEIGHT—double knitting and worsted yarns fall into this category, and are very popular. Double knitting stitch yield: 21–24. Needle size: 5–6 (3.75–4 mm). Worsted stitch yield: 16–20. Needle size: 7–9 (4.5–5.5 mm).

✳ HEAVY WEIGHT—Aran and chunky yarns are classed as "heavy weight." Stitch yield: 12–15. Needle size: 9–11 (5.5–8 mm).

✳ BULKY—there are lots of heavy novelty yarns available now. They are especially popular because they knit up very quickly. Stitch yield: 6–11. Needle size: 13–19 (9–16 mm).

GETTiNG STARTED

If you have never knitted before, the "basics"—how to hold the needles and yarn—may seem a little awkward. However, it will get easier with practice!

HOLDING THE NEEDLES

Holding the needles and yarn correctly is the first step toward professional-looking results. You can then proceed to cast on your first row.

1 Right hand—control the tip of the knitting needle with the thumb, index finger and middle finger. The other fingers stabilize the needle as you work.

2 Left hand—hold the needle in a similar way to that with your right hand.

HOLDING THE YARN

1 Pass the yarn over your right index finger, under the middle finger, over the ring finger and around your little finger. As you knit, the index finger is able to manipulate the yarn while the little finger controls the tension.

NOTE For left handers, simply reverse the holding positions.

MAKING A SLIP KNOT

Now you're ready to start. The first step is to anchor the yarn to the needle with a slip knot. This counts as the first stitch of your cast-on row.

1 Unwind a few yards of yarn from the ball and hold it in your left hand—this end of the yarn is called a "tail." Wind the yarn twice around your index and middle fingers. Use the tip of a knitting needle to pull the first strand through the second.

2 Pull the strand gently to form a loop, then adjust the tail and the yarn attached to the ball, called "the working yarn," so the loop fits snugly around the needle.

SIMPLE CASTING ON
USING THE THUMB METHOD

This simple method is used to create a neat but elastic row of stitches that form the basis of your knitted piece.

1 Make a slip knot, and hold the needle in your right hand. Loop the tail around your left thumb as shown, then hold the remaining yarn firmly against your palm using your ring finger and little finger.

2 Place the point of your needle into the loop formed around your thumb.

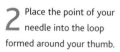

3 Now pass the working yarn around the point of the needle to form the next stitch.

4 Pull the new stitch through the loop and release the yarn from your thumb. Adjust the stitch so it sits snugly on the needle. Repeat until you have the number of stitches required.

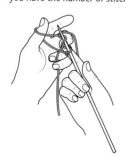
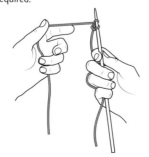

ABBREVIATIONS

Here is a list of the abbreviations you'll see in the patterns.

approx—approximately
BEG—beginning
COL—color
CM(S)—centimeter(s)
CONT—continue
DEC—decrease
DK—double knit
EV—every
FOLL— following
G ST—garter stitch
INC—increase
INC 1 st—increase by one stitch
K—knit
K2TOG—knit 2 stitches together
MEAS—measures
MM—millimeters
P—purl
P2TOG—purl 2 stitches together
PATT—pattern
PREV—previous
REM—remaining
REP—repeat
REV ST ST—reverse stocking stitch
RS—right side
ST OR STS—stitch or stitches
ST ST—stocking stitch
TOG—together
WRK—work
WS—wrong side
YO OR WRN—yarn over or wool around needle
* ASTERISK—repeat instructions between asterisks
( ) PARENTHESES—-repeat instructions in
parentheses the required number of times

BASIC STITCHES

Once you have the required number of stitches on your needle you will be keen to start knitting. First you must learn two basic stitches, the knit stitch and the purl stitch.

THE KNIT STITCH

1 Grasp the needle holding the cast-on stitches in your left hand and hold the other needle in your right hand. Place the point of the right-hand needle through the first cast-on stitch, from front to back.

2 Take up the working yarn in your right hand and guide it around the point of the right-hand needle.

3 Draw the resulting loop back gently through the first stitch.

4 Ease the right-hand needle away from the work slightly to allow the first stitch of the cast-on row to slip off the left-hand needle.

5 Repeat steps 1 to 4, knitting all the cast-on stitches until you reach the end. All the stitches will now have been transferred from the left-hand needle to the right-hand needle.

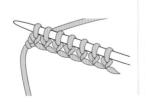

THE PURL STITCH

1 Now hold the needle with the stitches in your left hand to begin the purl row. Place the point of your right-hand needle through the first stitch from back to front.

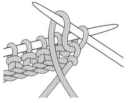

2 Guide the working yarn around the point of the right-hand needle using the index finger of your right hand.

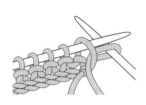

3 Draw the resulting loop back through the first stitch carefully to form the beginning of the purl row.

4 Ease the right-hand needle away from the work slightly to allow the first stitch of the cast-on row to slip off the left-hand needle.

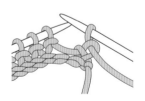

5 Repeat steps 1 to 4, purling all stitches until you reach the end. All the stitches will now have been transferred from the left-hand needle to the right-hand needle.

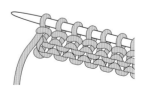

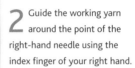
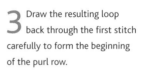
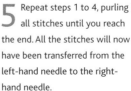

RIBBING

Now you have mastered knit and purl, you may proceed to the rib stitch, which is simply knit and purl stitches worked alternately. Bands of rib are most often used at the beginning of a knitted piece and for neckbands and button bands.

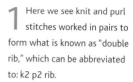

SINGLE RIB

One knit stitch and one purl stitch are worked alternately to form "single rib," which can be abbreviated to: k1 p1 rib.

1 Work from the cast-on row. Knit the first stitch, then bring the working yarn to the front between the first and second stitch.

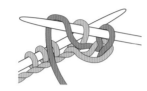

2 Purl the second stitch, then take the working yarn to the back between the second and third stitch.

3 Continue in this way, knitting and purling alternately until you reach the end of the row. For the next row, purl all the knit stitches and knit the purled stitches.

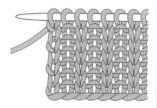

STOCKING STITCH

This is formed by alternating rows of knit stitch and purl stitch.

GARTER STITCH

This is formed with repeated rows of knit stitches only.

DOUBLE RIB

1 Here we see knit and purl stitches worked in pairs to form what is known as "double rib," which can be abbreviated to: k2 p2 rib.

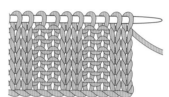

TENSION SAMPLE

Make a tension sample before you start your project. Using the needles suggested in the pattern, knit a swatch about 5 in (12.5 cm) square of stocking stitch. Now mark 4 in (10 cm) both horizontally and vertically with pins as shown. Count the rows and stitches to make sure they match the pattern suggestion. If not, use a larger or smaller needle size.

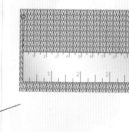

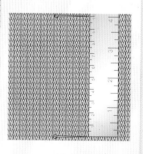

iNCREASiNG AND DECREASiNG

To shape your knitted pieces you will need to increase and decrease the number of stitches on your needle. All the pattern instructions use one stitch increases and decreases, usually positioned one or two stitches in from the edge of the piece.

INCREASING BY ONE STITCH

1 In a knit row, knit to the point of increase (your pattern will indicate the number of stitches). Knit the next stitch but do not slip it off the needle. Instead, knit into the back of it as shown to create a new stitch. Now slip the double stitch off the needle in the usual way.

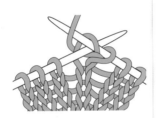

2 In a purl row, purl to the point of increase (your pattern will indicate the number of stitches). Purl the next stitch but do not slip it off the needle. Instead, take the yarn to the back of the work then knit into the back of the stitch. Slip the double stitch off the needle.

DECREASING BY ONE STITCH

Decreasing by one stitch can be abbreviated to: dec 1 st, or k2tog or p2tog (knit 2 together/purl 2 together).

1 In a knit row, work to the point of decrease, then knit the next two stitches together. This will cause a visible slant to the right on the right side of the work.

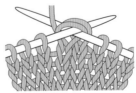

2 In a purl row, work to the point of decrease, then purl two stitches together. This causes a visible slant to the right on the right side of the work.

TIP

When decreasing, use the above method at the start of a row and the following method (slip stitch decrease, page 15) at the end of a row.

THE SLIP STITCH DECREASE

This method of decreasing by one stitch can be used instead of working two stitches together. It also creates a visible slant on the right side of a knit row, but this time to the left.

1 Knit to the point of decrease, then slip the next stitch onto the right-hand needle without knitting it. Knit the next stitch as usual.

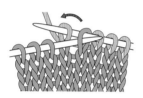

2 Now, using the tip of the left-hand needle, pick up the slipped stitch and pass it over the last knitted one, thus losing a stitch. Continue to the end of the row as usual.

SEWING IN TAILS

At various points in your knitting you will need to join on a new ball of yarn or change color. This operation leaves dangling ends or "tails" on the wrong side. Avoid the temptation to ignore them; sew them in for a neat finish.

1 Thread the "tail" onto a bodkin and work it into the ridges of the stitches on the wrong side, in a wavy line.

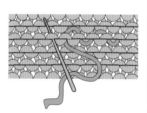

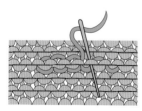

2 For extra security, work the tail back along the row then snip off the yarn no less than ½ in (1.5 cm) from the knitted work.

BINDING OFF

When you come to the end of a knitted piece, the stitches have to be finished to prevent the whole thing from unraveling! This is called binding off or casting off. Follow the next four diagrams for a neat finish in knit and purl rows.

BINDING/CASTING OFF KNITWISE

1 Knit the first two stitches, then, using the point of your left-hand needle, pick up the first stitch and pass it over the second.

2 You have now cast off one stitch. Continue in this way until you reach the last stitch. Snip off the working yarn and pull it through the last stitch to secure the cast-off edge.

BINDING/CASTING OFF PURLWISE

1 Purl the first two stitches, then, using the point of your left-hand needle, pick up the first stitch and pass it over the second.

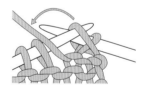

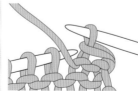

2 You have now cast off one stitch. Continue in this way until you reach the last stitch. Snip off the working yarn and pull it through the last stitch to secure the cast-off edge.

USING MORE THAN ONE COLOR

Introducing patterns, large areas of color, or more than one color in the same row is not as complicated as it may first appear. You will see colored charts included with your knitting instructions. These are used for creating patterns and motifs. These three methods require a certain amount of manual dexterity but remember—practice makes perfect!

FAIR ISLE

The Fair Isle method can be used if the colors you intend to add in the row do not exceed three or four stitches at a time. The yarn need not be cut and joined separately for every color change, but carried loosely across the work at the back. These strands are called "floats."

1 Knit your work to the beginning of the patterned area then introduce yarn in a contrasting color. Work the required number of stitches in the contrast color, then change back to the original color.

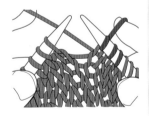

2 Strand the original yarn loosely across the back of your work while you use the contrast color, then do likewise with the contrast color as you work the original yarn. Getting the tension correct can be tricky, but will get easier with practice.

INTARSIA

This method creates larger areas of color without the need for "floats" at the back. Each area is knitted using a separate ball of yarn. The yarns are twisted together on the wrong side of each intersection so your work holds together in one piece!

DIAGONAL COLOR CHANGES

For changes to the left or right, work one stitch more or less in the original color before changing to the contrast yarn.

1 For a color change leading to the left on the right side, work one more stitch in yarn A, then drop it to the back. Pick up yarn B and take it under and over yarn A. Continue stitching.

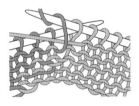

2 For a color change leading to the right on the right side, work one less stitch in yarn A, then continue in the contrast yarn B. The two yarns will link on the wrong side.

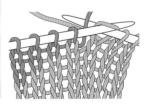

VERTICAL COLOR CHANGES

Yarns are still linked on the wrong side when changing color in a vertical direction. (Color changes can also be made along horizontal lines.)

1 On the right side—work the required number of stitches in yarn A, then allow it to fall over yarn B at the back. Take up yarn B and work the required stitches, then change back to yarn A. Remember to use separate balls of yarn each time.

2 On the wrong side—the required number of stitches have been worked in yarn A, then changed to yarn B, then changed back to A. Notice how the yarns have been twisted on the back to prevent holes from forming.

SWISS EMBROIDERY / DARNING

Swiss embroidery or darning is sometimes referred to as "duplicate stitch." It's a simple handworked embroidery stitch that imitates stocking stitch on the right side of a knitted piece and is used to add areas of color.

1 Thread your contrast color on a bodkin and secure the end on the wrong side. Bring the point of the needle to the right side at the base of the first stitch of the area to be decorated. Insert the needle under the base of the next stitch above.

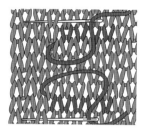

2 Reinsert the needle into the base of the first stitch to form the first embroidered stitch. Continue in this way to complete the pattern.

TIP

Swiss embroidery can be used instead of the Intarsia method for adding color and pattern to your knitted pieces.

FINISHING YOUR DOGGY GARMENT

When you have completed the knitted pieces, all that remains is for you to finish them neatly and join them together. Take time to do this carefully in order to achieve a good result.

PICKING UP STITCHES ON A SHAPED EDGE

Most garments need a neckband. This requires picking up stitches around the neckline in order to knit the band onto it.

1 Check your pattern to see how many stitches you need to pick up. Mark the center with a pin so you can pick up

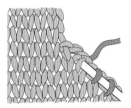

stitches evenly. Insert the tip of the needle through the work from the right side, then draw the yarn from the back to the front to form a loop. Keep the loop on the needle and repeat to pick up another stitch. Continue until you have the required number of stitches on your needle. Continue working the band in rib stitch or as directed.

ATTACHING A BUTTON/BUTTONHOLE BAND

Separate button and buttonhole bands are simply long, narrow pieces of rib that are stitched to the front or back opening of a garment.

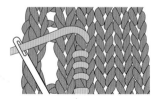

1 Place the knitted bands next to the opening and oversew the edge of the band to the edge of the garment neatly.

EYELET BUTTONHOLE

This is an easy way to make a small buttonhole, and can be worked as part of the main garment or in a ribbed buttonhole band. The eyelet is started in one row and then completed in the next row.

1 Knit or rib to the buttonhole position as directed in your knitting pattern, then form the eyelet as follows. Take the working yarn forward around the needle then back to the original knitting position—abbreviated to wrn (wool around needle) or yo (yarn over). Now knit the next two stitches together.

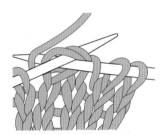

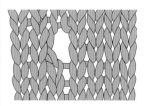

2 For the next row, work across all stitches in purl or rib as directed. You will see that a small hole has formed in the buttonhole position.

STITCHING PIECES TOGETHER

Many well-knitted garments have been ruined by poor sewing practice. Lumpy or distorted seams do not look good on any garment! Here are three methods to help you sew your knitted pieces together successfully.

THE FLAT SEAM

This seam is strong and neat, and is often used to join ribbed bands or garter-stitched pieces together.

1 Place the pieces to be joined together with right sides facing. Thread a bodkin with matching yarn and secure it to the right-hand edge as shown.

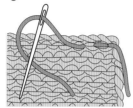

2 Hold the knitted pieces in your left hand, placing your index finger between the two layers. Pass the bodkin from one piece through the next in a zigzag fashion as shown, working slowly stitch by stitch.

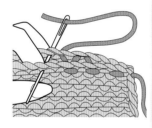

3 From the right side your seam should resemble this diagram. Try to match the stitches from both pieces neatly to make the seam as inconspicuous as possible.

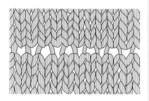

THE BACKSTITCH SEAM

If elasticity in the seam is not required, then the backstitch seam is used.

1 Place the knitted pieces with right sides together. You may use pins to secure the pieces if necessary. Thread a bodkin with matching yarn and secure it to the right-hand edge. Join the seam using a neat backstitch, as shown.

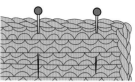

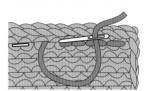

THE INVISIBLE SEAM

The invisible seam is quite tricky to accomplish, but results in a neat, elastic, and almost invisible seam—hence the name!

1 Place the pieces to be joined right side up. Thread a bodkin with matching yarn and secure it on the wrong side of the lower edge of the right-hand piece. Bring the yarn through to the right side.

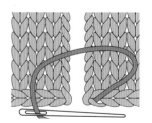

2 Pick up the center strand of the first stitch at the lower edge of the left-hand piece. Now pick up a stitch in the same way on the right-hand piece, then return to the other side.

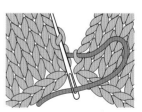

3 Work carefully along the seam, picking up one stitch at a time from each side. Pull the sewing yarn very gently as you go so the pieces come together neatly and securely.

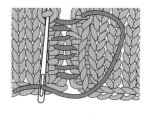

SALTY SEA DOG

SET SAIL IN STYLE

Ahoy there land lubbers! Shiver me timbers, splice the mainbrace, dance the hornpipe, and hoist the mainsail! Phew, that sounds like too much seafaring activity for our salty sea dog— a quick stroll around the block will probably keep him happy. This crisp navy-and-white nautical number, complete with little sailor hat, is knitted in smooth pure cotton double-knit yarn: fully washable, cool, and comfortable to wear.

YOU WILL NEED

pair of US size 4 (3.5 mm) needles

pair of US size 6 (4 mm) needles

3 [4:6] x 1½ oz (50 g) balls of DK cotton yarn
in color A (white)

2 [1:1] x 1½ oz (50 g) ball of DK cotton yarn
in color B (navy blue)

stitch holder

tape measure

safety pins

US size 6 (4 mm) circular needle

skein of embroidery thread in color C (red)

bodkin

glass-headed pins

20 in (50 cm) length of ¼ in (5 mm)
wide black elastic

scissors

KEY COLOR A—DK COTTON YARN, WHITE
COLOR B—DK COTTON YARN, NAVY BLUE
COLOR C—EMBROIDERY THREAD, RED

It's a life on the ocean wave for me—just don't get my outfit wet!

KNiTTiNG UP

SPECIAL ABBREVIATIONS

(See page 11 for general abbreviations.)

Border patt—wrk 2 rows in col A, 2 rows in col B, 2 rows in col A, 2 rows in col B.

TENSION

22 sts and 30 rows measured over a 4 x 4 in (10 x 10 cm) square of stocking stitch, worked on US size 6 (4 mm) needles.

BACK

Using US size 4 (3.5 mm) needles and col B, cast on 62 [88:114] sts.
K 3 rows.
Change to col A and US size 6 (4 mm) needles, then cont in st st, following border patt and colors until wrk meas 5½ [8:10½] in (14 [20:26] cm) from cast-on edge.

ARMHOLE SHAPING

Bind off 2 [2:3] sts at beg of next 2 rows, dec 1 st at both ends of next, then ev foll 3 [2:2] rows 1 [3:4] times. 54 [76:98] sts rem.
Cont until wrk meas 11 [16: 20½] in (28 [40:52] cm) from cast-on edge, ending after a ws row.
Place all the sts on stitch holder for back neck.
Measure 2¾ [4:5] in (7 [10:13] cm) down each side from top of work. Then mark these two points with safety pins to indicate how far to stitch the front shoulder along the back armhole edge.

FRONT

Using US size 4 (3.5 mm) needles and col B, cast on 54 [78:98] sts.
K 3 rows.
Change to col A and US size 6 (4 mm) needles and cont in st st, following border patt and colors until wrk meas 5½ [8:10½] in (14 [20:26] cm) from cast-on edge.

ARMHOLE SHAPING

Bind off 2 [2:3] sts at beg of next 2 rows, dec 1 st at both ends of next, then ev foll 3 [2:2] rows 2 [4:5] times. 44 [64:80] sts rem.
Cont until wrk meas 7 [10:13] in (18 [25:33] cm) from cast-on edge, ending after a ws row.

DIVIDE FOR NECK/COLLAR

Next row: with rs facing, work 22 [33:41] sts, then slip rem 22 [33:41] sts onto a stitch holder.
Cont on these sts for left front.

With ws facing cont as follows:
Using col B cast on 2 [3:4] sts at center front and k them. Then k 2 [3:4] more sts. Change to col A and p rem sts.
Wrk 2 rows, using st st for col A sts, and rev st st and garter st for col B sts.
4th row, wrk 19 [29:36] sts in col A. Change to col B, p1 and k rem sts.
5th row, k 5 [7:9] sts, change to col A and cont in st st to end.
You will see a 1 st diagonal color change in col B from the center to the outside edge.
Continue in this way, moving 1 st in col B ev 3 [3:3] rows, 9 [1:13] times, then ev 0 [4:4] rows 0 [11:4] times.
Cont without diagonal color change until wrk meas 11 [16:20½] in (28 [40:52] cm) from cast-on edge, ending after a ws row.

SHOULDER SHAPING

Bind off 2 [2:2] sts at beg of next and ev alt row 4 [8:11] times.

Place rem sts on stitch holder for left front neck/collar.

RIGHT FRONT/COLLAR

With rs facing, return to the sts held on st holder.

Using col B cast on 2 [3:4] sts, k 2 sts, change to col A then k rem sts.

Wrk diagonal color change and garter st edge as for left front but reverse the direction of the color change.

Cont right front shoulder shaping as left but reverse the shapings.

Place sts on stitch holder for right front neck/collar.

 COLLAR

Work with rs of all pieces facing.

Pin the outside edge of the left and right front shoulders to the markers on the back armhole edges. Stitch the shoulders in place.

With rs facing, slip all sts held on stitch holders at right front neck, back neck, and left front neck onto a US size 6 (4 mm) circular needle. Cont in rev st st in col B, keeping the 4 [4:6] sts of garter st at the two front edges until wrk meas 4 [6:8] in (10 [15:20] cm) from the base of the back neck and ending after a ws row. Now work 2 rows col A, 2 rows col B, 2 rows col A, two rows col B. K 3 rows in col A then bind off all sts.

 SLEEVES (MAKE TWO)

Using US size 4 (3.5 mm) needles and col B, cast on 30 [45:59] sts.

K 3 rows.

Change to col A and US size 6 (4 mm) needles and cont in st st, following border patt and colors.

SLEEVE SHAPING

Inc 1 st at both ends of next, then of ev foll 3 [2:3] rows 11 [10:19] times, then ev foll 0 [4:0] rows 0 [6:0] times. 54 [79:99] sts rem.

Cont without shaping until wrk meas 8 [10½:12¾] in (20 [26:32] cm) from cast-on edge (or work to specific dog measurements), ending after a ws row. Bind off all sts.

 TIE

Using US size 4 (3.5 mm) needles and col B cast on 4 sts and work garter stitch for 8 [12:16] in (20 [30:40] cm) then bind off.

 HAT

Using US size 4 (3.5 mm) needles and col B, cast on 56 sts.

Work 3 rows of garter stitch.

Change to US size 6 (4 mm) needles and cont in st st.

For the border pattern work 2 rows in col A, 2 rows in col B, 2 rows in col A, 2 rows in col B. Cont in col A until wrk meas 4¾ in (12 cm) from cast-on edge, ending with a ws row.

SHAPING

1st row, k 1, *k2tog, k3*.

Rep from * to *. 45 sts rem.

2nd row, p to end.

3rd row, k 1, *k2tog, k2*.

Rep from * to *. 34 sts rem.

4th row, p to end.

5th row, k 1, *k2tog, k1*. Rep from * to *. 23 sts rem.

6th row, p to end.

7th row, k1, *K2tog*. Rep from * to *. 12 sts rem.

8th row, p to end.

9th row, *K2tog*. Rep from * to *. 6 sts rem.

10th row, p to end.

Break off yarn and pass it through last 6 sts. Then draw up tightly.

 MOTIF FOR SLEEVES

Using col B and Swiss embroidery technique (see page 17) work anchor motif from chart below onto both sleeves. Mark the center row with pins before stitching, counting the rows and stitches carefully from the chart.

MAKING UP

 TOP

1 Join the neckband.

2 Join the side seams and sleeve seams.

3 Place a marker pin halfway along each front armhole. Then pin the sleeve seams to the markers and stitch the sleeves into the armholes.

NECKLINE

1 Turn the sailor costume to the wrong side.

2 Slip stitch the loose edge of the lower welt to the garment at the base of the welt using col B.

3 Take the end of the sewing yarn through to the right side ready to sew on the tie.

TIE

➡ **1** Fold the garter stitch tie in half, then place the fold at the base of the neck welt.
2 Open up the tie and secure in place with a few stitches either side using col B.
3 Take the end of the thread to the wrong side and finish off neatly.

🐾 HAT

1 Thread the tail at the top of the hat onto a bodkin, then use it to join the crown seam.
2 Stitch a short length of elastic onto the hat as a chin strap. Measure the dog's head first to ensure a snug, but not tight, fit.

POM POM

⬅ **1** Cut about 30 x 2 in (5 cm) lengths of yarn in col A. Tie another length of yarn tightly around the center then stitch the bundle to the top of the hat.

FRENCH COUTURE

THINK PINK

Ooh, la la! Our little friend wears this outfit with tremendous poise! This neat jacket with dark bindings is a homage to the great fashion designer Chanel who created this classic look—the cute beret is an absolute must as a finishing touch! Why not add a pearl-embellished collar and leash just for authenticity?

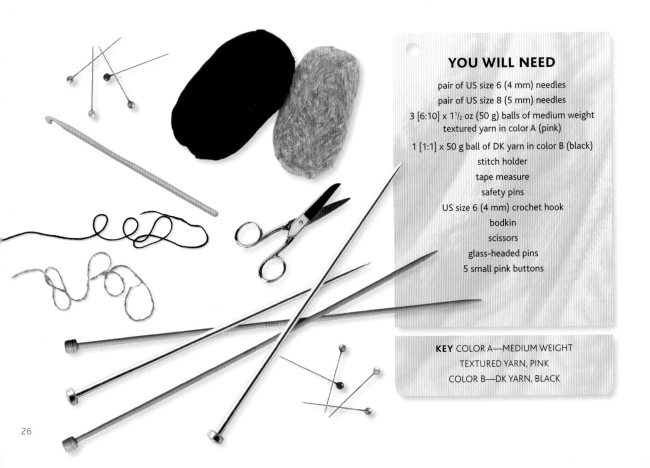

YOU WILL NEED

pair of US size 6 (4 mm) needles
pair of US size 8 (5 mm) needles
3 [6:10] x 1½ oz (50 g) balls of medium weight textured yarn in color A (pink)
1 [1:1] x 50 g ball of DK yarn in color B (black)
stitch holder
tape measure
safety pins
US size 6 (4 mm) crochet hook
bodkin
scissors
glass-headed pins
5 small pink buttons

KEY COLOR A—MEDIUM WEIGHT TEXTURED YARN, PINK
COLOR B—DK YARN, BLACK

KNiTTiNG UP

 SPECIAL ABBREVIATIONS

(See page 11 for general abbreviations.)

REV ST ST—reverse stocking stitch. Knit and purl rows are worked alternately but the purl side is the right side.

 TENSION

17 sts and 24 rows measured over a 4 x 4 in (10 x 10 cm) square of stocking stitch, worked on US size 8 (5 mm) needles.

 BACK

Using US size 6 (4 mm) needles and col A, cast on 48 [68:88] sts.

Wrk rev st st for 1¹/₂ in (4 cm).

Change to US size 8 (5 mm) needles and cont in rev st st.

Cont until wrk meas 5¹/₂ [8:10¹/₂] in (14 [20:26] cm) from cast-on edge.

ARMHOLE SHAPING

Bind off 2 sts at beg of next 2 rows, dec 1 st at both ends of next, then ev alt row 0 [1:2] times. 42 [60:78] sts rem. Cont in rev st st until wrk meas 11 [15¹/₂:20¹/₂] in (28 [40:52] cm) from cast-on edge, ending after a ws row.

Place all stitches on stitch holder for back neck.

Now meas 2¹/₂ [4:5] in (7 [10:13] cm) down each side (armhole) edge from top of work. Mark these two points with safety pins or short lengths of yarn to indicate how far to stitch the front shoulder along the back armhole/shoulder edge.

 LEFT FRONT

Using US size 6 (4 mm) needles and col A, cast on 20 [30:40] sts.

Wrk rev st st for 1¹/₂ in (4 cm).

Change to US size 8 (5 mm) needles.

Cont in rv st st until wrk meas 5¹/₂ [8:10¹/₂] in (14 [20:26] cm) from cast-on edge.

ARMHOLE SHAPING

Bind off 2 sts at beg of next row, wrk 1 row, then dec 1 st at beg of next and then ev alt row 0 [1:2] times. 17 [26:35] sts rem. Cont in rev st st until wrk meas 11 [15¹/₂:20¹/₂] in (28 [39:52] cm) from cast-on edge, ending after a ws row.

SHOULDER SHAPING

Bind off 2 sts at beg of next then at same end of ev alt row 3 [5:7] times. 9 [14:19] sts rem.

Place all stitches on stitch holder for front neck.

 RIGHT FRONT

Follow same instructions but reverse the shoulder shaping.

 SLEEVE (MAKE TWO)

Using US size 6 (4 mm) needles and col A, cast on 24 [34:44] sts.

Wrk rev st st for 1¹/₂ in (4 cm).

Change to US size 8 (5 mm) needles.

SLEEVE SHAPING

Inc 1 st at both ends of next then ev 3 [3:3] rows 7 [12:15] times. You now have 40 [60:76] sts.

Cont without shaping until wrk meas 8 [10¹/₂:12¹/₂] in (20 [26:32] cm) from cast-on edge (or to specific dog measurements) ending after a ws row. Bind off all sts.

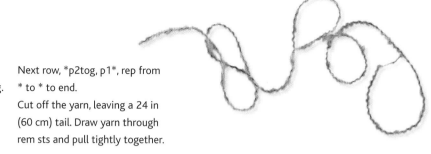

NECKBAND

Work with right side of all pieces facing.

Using US size 6 (4 mm) needles and col A, pick up and purl the stitches held at right front, back neck, then left front neck.
Wrk rev st st for 1½ in (4 cm), ending with a ws row.
Next row, bind off all sts.

 HAT

Using US size 6 (4 mm) needles and col B, cast on 50 sts.
Wrk rev st st for 1 in (2.5 cm), ending after a ws row.
Change to US size 8 (5 mm) needles and cont in rev st st foll crown shaping.

CROWN SHAPING

Next row *p2, inc 1*, rep from * to * to last 2 sts and p to end.
You will now have 66 sts.
Cont without shaping for a further 1½ in (4 cm), ending after a ws row.
Next row, *p2tog, p4*, rep from * to * to end.
P all sts.
Next row, *p2tog, p3*, rep from * to * to end.
P all sts.
Next row, *p2tog, p2*, rep from * to * to end.
P all sts.

Next row, *p2tog, p1*, rep from * to * to end.
Cut off the yarn, leaving a 24 in (60 cm) tail. Draw yarn through rem sts and pull tightly together.

With the crochet hook work 10 chains using the yarn tail, then pull the yarn through the last chain. Fold the chain in half and, using a bodkin, secure the tail to the first chain. This makes a little decorative loop at the top of the beret.

I simply can't be seen out on the sidewalk without my pink designer suit!

Making up

🐾 JACKET

1 Pin the outside edges of the left and right front shoulders to the markers on the back armhole edges. Stitch the shoulders in place.
2 Join the side seams and sleeve seams.
3 Place a marker pin halfway along each front armhole. Then pin the sleeve seams to the markers, and stitch the sleeves into the armholes.

🐾 CROCHET TRIM

1 Using a US size 6 (4 mm) crochet hook and col B, work two rows of single crochet around the cast-on edge of each of the sleeves.
2 Crochet a single row around the hem, neckline, and front edges of the jacket.
3 Use pins to indicate the position of five evenly spaced buttonholes along the right front edge.
4 Work a second row of crochet as the first but with a buttonhole at each pin-marked position (*see page 31*).
◄ **5** Stitch five buttons to the left front edge of the jacket to correspond with each buttonhole.

MAKING A CROCHET CHAIN

1 Make a slip loop. Thread your yarn in your left hand and hold the crochet hook with the slip loop in the right hand. Twist the crochet hook first under and then over the yarn to make a loop.

2 Draw the hook and yarn through the slip loop.

MAKING A CROCHET BUTTONHOLE

1 Work from the side edge to the buttonhole position (about 3 or 4 stitches in). Make two or more chains, depending on the size of your button. Miss the same number of stitches in the row below.

2 Re-insert your hook and work in pattern to the end of the row. On the following row, work in pattern over the chains.

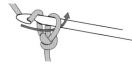 **HAT**

➡ **1** Thread the tail at the top of the beret onto a bodkin, then use it to join the crown seam together.

⬅ **2** Using a US size 6 (4 mm) crochet hook and col B, work two rows of single crochet around the cast-on edge of the hat.

BUZZY BEE

BEE BEAUTIFUL

Buzz, buzz, buzz... Our cute and cuddly little busy, buzzy bee outfit is particularly suitable for small dogs. It is easily and quickly knitted up in a fabulous shaggy-style yarn that perfectly emulates the fluffiness of a real bee. Top it off with a tiny hat with pipe cleaner antennae, then add some delicate wings to complete the look. You can buy ready-made fairy wings from a fancy dress store—why make life difficult for yourself? This is meant to be fun after all!

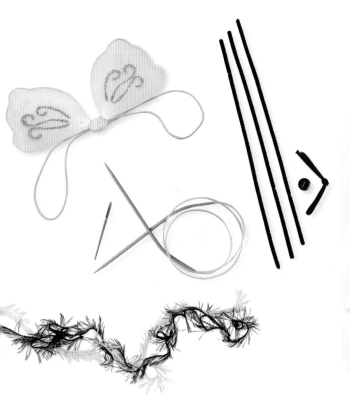

YOU WILL NEED

pair of US size 6 (4 mm) needles
pair of US size 4 (3.5 mm) needles
2 [3:4] x 1½ oz (50 g) balls of fur-effect yarn in color A (black)
2 [3:4] x 1½ oz (50 g) balls of fur-effect yarn in color B (yellow)
stitch holder
tape measure
safety pins
bodkin
sewing needle
sewing thread
scissors
glass-headed pins
2 thick black pipe cleaners
pair of child's fairy wings
¼ in (5 mm wide) black elastic (length cut to fit)

KEY COLOR A—FUR-EFFECT YARN, BLACK
COLOR B—FUR-EFFECT YARN, YELLOW

KNiTTiNG UP

🐾 SPECIAL ABBREVIATIONS

(See page 11 for general abbreviations.)

PATT—8 rows col A, 8 rows col B.

🐾 TENSION

22 sts and 32 rows measured over a 4 x 4 in (10 x 10 cm) square of stocking stitch, worked on US size 6 (4 mm) needles.

🐾 BACK

Using US size 4 (3.5 mm) needles and col B, cast on 62 [88:114] sts.

Cont in patt throughout.

Wrk k1 p1 rib for 1½ in (4 cm), ending after a ws row.

Change to US size 6 (4 mm) needles.

Cont in st st and patt until wrk meas 5½ [8:10½] in (14 [20:26] cm) from cast-on edge.

ARMHOLE SHAPING

Bind off 2 [2:3] sts at beg of next 2 rows, dec 1 st at both ends of next, then ev foll 3 [2:2] rows 1 [3:4] times.

Cont in patt until wrk meas 11 [16:20½] in (28 [40:52] cm) from cast-on edge, ending after a ws row.

Place all rem stitches on stitch holder for back neck.

Measure 2¾ [4:5] in (7 [10:13] cm) down each side from top of work. Then mark these two points with safety pins to indicate how far to stitch the front shoulder along the back armhole edge.

🐾 FRONT

Using US size 4 (3.5 mm) needles and col B, cast on 62 [88:114] sts.

Cont in patt throughout.

Wrk k1 p1 rib for 1½ in (4 cm), ending after a ws row.

Change to US size 6 (4 mm) needles.

Cont in st st and patt until wrk meas 5½ [8:10½] in (14 [20:26] cm) from cast-on edge.

ARMHOLE SHAPING

Bind off 2 [2:3] sts at beg of next 2 rows, dec 1 st at both ends of next, then ev foll 3 [2:2] rows 1 [3:4] times. 54 [76:98] sts rem.

Continue in patt until wrk meas 11 [16: 20½] in (28 [40:52] cm) from cast-on edge, ending after a ws row.

SHOULDER SHAPING

Bind off 2 [2:2] sts at beg of next 12 [16:20] rows. 30 [44:58] sts rem.

Place remaining sts on stitch holder for front neck.

🐾 SLEEVES (MAKE TWO)

Using US size 4 (3.5 mm) needles and col B, cast on 30 [45:59] sts.

Cont in patt throughout.

Wrk k1 p1 rib for 1½ in (4 cm), ending after a ws row.

Change to US size 6 (4 mm) needles and cont in st st and patt.

SLEEVE SHAPING

Inc 1 st at both ends of next, then of ev foll 3 [2:3] rows 11 [10:19] times, then every foll 0 [4:0] rows 0 [6:0] times. 54 [79:99] sts rem.

Cont without shaping until wrk meas 8 [10$\frac{1}{2}$:12$\frac{3}{4}$] in (20 [26:32] cm) from cast-on edge (or work to specific dog measurement), ending after a ws row. Bind off all sts.

🐾 HAT

Using US size 4 (3.5 mm) needles and col B, cast on 36 sts.

Cont in st st until wrk measures 2 in (5 cm) from cast-on edge, ending after a ws row.

CROWN SHAPING

1st row, *k2tog*, rep from * to * to end.

P 1 row.

3rd row, rep 1st row.

Break off the yarn, leaving a tail of approx 8 in (20 cm) in length.

Thread the tail onto a bodkin. Then pass the yarn through the last stitches and draw up tightly.

🐾 NECKBAND

Work with rs of all pieces facing.

Using US size 4 (3.5 mm) needles and col B, pick up and knit the sts held at front and back neck.

Wrk k1 p1 rib for 1$\frac{1}{2}$ in (4 cm), ending with a ws row.

Next row bind off all sts loosely.

MAKING UP

SWEATER

1 Join the neckband.

2 Pin the outside edges of the left and right front shoulders to the markers on the back armhole edges. Stitch the shoulders in place.

3 Join the side seams and sleeve seams.

4 Place a marker pin halfway along each front armhole. Then pin the sleeve seams to the markers, and stitch the sleeves into the armholes.

WINGS

 1 Wind a few strands of yarn around the center of the fairy wings to disguise the fabric and the ends of the wires.

HAT

1 Thread the yarn tail onto a bodkin and use it to stitch the hat seam, finishing securely.

ANTENNAE

⇐ **1** To make the antennae, place the two pipe cleaners side by side and twist them together loosely. Bend each end into a small loop. Then bend both the pipe cleaners into a "U" shape.

→ 2 Stitch the center of the antennae to the top part of the hat using col A.

← 3 Using matching sewing thread, stitch a length of elastic to the hat as a chin strap. Measure the dog first so that the strap is secure but comfortable.

SUPERHERO

THE SKY'S THE LIMIT

"Is it a bird, is it a plane?—no it's Superdog!" He can leap tall buildings in a single bound too! This is an outfit where you can really ring the changes: the basic caped shape can be given a completely different character simply by changing the color combinations. Choose your favorite superhero and adjust the color scheme to match. For added "superhero-ness" you could add an eyemask, too. "Up, up, and away!"

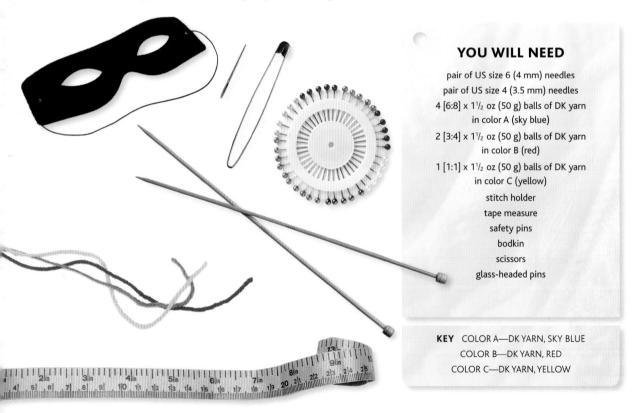

YOU WILL NEED

pair of US size 6 (4 mm) needles
pair of US size 4 (3.5 mm) needles
4 [6:8] x 1½ oz (50 g) balls of DK yarn
in color A (sky blue)
2 [3:4] x 1½ oz (50 g) balls of DK yarn
in color B (red)
1 [1:1] x 1½ oz (50 g) balls of DK yarn
in color C (yellow)
stitch holder
tape measure
safety pins
bodkin
scissors
glass-headed pins

KEY COLOR A—DK YARN, SKY BLUE
COLOR B—DK YARN, RED
COLOR C—DK YARN, YELLOW

KNiTTiNG UP

SPECIAL ABBREVIATIONS

(See page 11 for general abbreviations.)

TENSION

22 sts and 30 rows measured over a 4 x 4 in (10 x 10 cm) square of stocking stitch, worked on US size 6 (4 mm) needles.

BACK

Using US size 4 (3.5 mm) needles and col A, cast on 62 [88:114] sts.

Wrk k1 p1 rib for 4 in (10 cm), ending after a ws row.

Change to US size 6 (4 mm) needles and col A.

Cont in st st until wrk meas 5¹/₂ [8:10¹/₂] in (14 [20:26] cm) from cast-on edge.

ARMHOLE SHAPING

Bind off 2 [2:3] sts at beg of next 2 rows, dec 1 st at both ends of next, then ev foll 3 [2:2] rows 1 [3:4] times. 54 [76:98] sts rem.

Cont until wrk meas 11 [16:20¹/₂] in (28 [40:52] cm) from cast-on edge, ending after a ws row.

Place all stitches on stitch holder for back neck.

Measure 2³/₄ [4:5] in (7 [10:13] cm) down each side from top of work. Then mark these two points with safety pins or short lengths of yarn to indicate how far to stitch the front shoulder along the back armhole edge.

FRONT

Using US size 4 (3.5 mm) needles and col A, cast on 62 [88:114] sts.

Wrk k1 p1 rib for 4 in (10 cm), ending after a ws row.

Change to US size 6 (4 mm) needles and col A.

Cont in st st until wrk meas 5¹/₂ [8:10¹/₂] in (14 [20:26] cm) from cast-on edge.

ARMHOLE SHAPING

Bind off 2 [2:3] sts at beg of next 2 rows, dec 1 st at both ends of next, then ev foll 3 [2:2] rows 1 [3:4] times.

MOTIF

Work the motif using the Intarsia method *(see pages 16–17)* using cols B and C. Count sts carefully and make sure the motif is centrally placed—the center is marked on the chart opposite. Alternatively, complete the garment front then work the motif afterward using the Swiss embroidery method *(see page 17)*.

Cont in st st until wrk meas 11 [16:20½] in (28 [40:52] cm) from cast-on edge, ending after a ws row.

SHOULDER SHAPING
Bind off 2 [2:2] sts at beg of next 12 [16:20] rows. 30 [44:58] sts remain. Place remaining sts on stitch holder for front neck.

SLEEVES (MAKE TWO)
Using US size 4 (3.5 mm) needles and col C, cast on 30 [44:59] sts.
Wrk k1 p1 rib for 1½ in (4 cm), ending

after a ws row.
Change to US size 6 (4 mm) needles and cont in st st.

SLEEVE SHAPING
Inc 1 st at both ends of next, then of ev foll 3 [2:3] rows 11 [10:19] times, then ev foll 0 [4:0] rows 0 [6:0] times. 54 (79:99) sts rem.
Cont without shaping until wrk meas 8 [10½:12¾] in (20 [26:32] cm) from cast-on edge (or work to specific dog measurements), ending after a ws row.
Bind off all sts.

NECKBAND
Work with rs of all pieces facing.
Using US size 4 (3.5 mm) needles and col A, pick up and knit the sts held at front and back neck.
Wrk k1 p1 rib for 1½ in (4 cm), ending with a ws row.
Next row bind off all sts.

BELT
Using US size 4 (3.5 mm) needles and col C, cast on 12 sts.
Cont in k1 p1 rib until belt meas 20 [28:36] in (50 [70:90] cm).
Bind off.

CAPE
Using US size 6 (4 mm) needles and col B, cast on 62 [88:114] sts.
Cont in garter st for 6 in (15 cm).
Dec 1 st at both ends of next row and then ev foll 8 [8:8] rows 3 [7:11] times.
Cont without shaping until wrk meas 11 [16:20½] in (28 [40:52] cm) from cast-on edge.
Bind off.

CENTER LINE

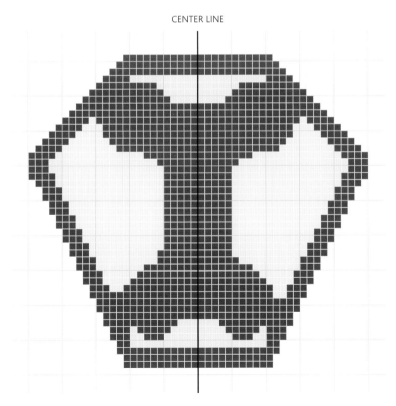

MAKING UP

🐾 SUPERHERO SUPER TOP

1 Join the neckband.

2 Pin the outside edges of the left and right front shoulders to the markers on the back armhole edges. Stitch the shoulders in place.

3 Join the side seams and sleeve seams.

4 Place a marker pin halfway along each front armhole. Then pin the sleeve seams to the markers, and stitch the sleeves into the armholes.

🐾 BELT

⬆ **1** Make belt loops using two strands of col B yarn threaded onto a bodkin. For each loop work two large stitches approximately $1\frac{1}{2}$ in (4 cm) long at the top of the ribbed band as shown. Position one loop at each side seam, then position two more on the front and the back, spacing them equally.

Don't take all day with that belt! There's a world out there waiting to be saved!

 2 Thread the yellow ribbed belt through the loops and join the short ends together at the back. The seam will be hidden when the cape is stitched on.

🐾 CAPE

➡ **1** Pin the upper edge of the cape to the base of the ribbed neckband at the back. Slip stitch the cape to the garment, taking care not to pull the stitches too tight so that the neckband remains elastic.

BELLBOY

GOING UP

"Ding, ding!" Our busy little bellboy certainly has his work cut out for him—all those suitcases to carry! This charming jacket and hat combo just had to be red, red, red... with gold tassels and trimmings, of course. A word of warning: make sure the frog fasteners are firmly attached—you don't want your doggy eating them for dinner!

YOU WILL NEED

pair of US size 8 (5 mm) needles
pair of US size 10 (6 mm) needles
2 [4:6] x 3½ oz (100 g) balls of chunky yarn in color A (red)
tape measure
stitch holder
safety pins
glass-headed pins
bodkin
sewing needle
sewing thread
scissors
2 yds [3:4] (2 [3:4] m) gold braid
5 gold frog fasteners
US size 6 (4 mm) crochet hook
1 x 1½ oz (50 g) ball metallic fingering in color B (gold)
20 in (50 cm) red or black ¼ in (5 mm) wide elastic for hat

KEY COLOR A—CHUNKY YARN, RED
COLOR B—METALLIC FINGERING, GOLD

KNiTTiNG UP

 SPECIAL ABBREVIATIONS

(See page 11 for general abbreviations.)

 TENSION

14 sts and 19 rows measured over a 4 x 4 in (10 x 10 cm) square of stocking stitch, worked on US size 10 (6 mm) needles.

 BACK

Using US size 8 (5 mm) needles and col A, cast on 40 [56:72] sts.
Wrk k1 p1 rib for 1$^1/_2$ in (4 cm), ending after a ws row.
Change to US size 10 (6 mm) needles.
Cont in st st until wrk meas 5$^1/_2$ [8:10$^1/_2$] in (14 [20:26] cm) from cast-on edge.

ARMHOLE SHAPING

Bind off 1 st at beg of next 2 rows, then dec 1 st at both ends of next, then ev alt row 1 [2:3] times.
34 [48:62] sts rem.
Cont in st st until wrk meas 11 [15$^1/_2$:20$^1/_2$] in (28 [40:52] cm) from cast-on edge, ending after a ws row.
Place stitches on a stitch holder for back neck.
Now meas 2$^3/_4$ [4:5] in (7 [10:13] cm) down each side edge from top of work. Mark these two points with safety pins to indicate how far to stitch the front shoulder seam along the back armhole/shoulder edge.

 CARDIGAN FRONT (LEFT)

Using US size 8 (5 mm) needles and col A, cast on 17 [24:31] sts.
Wrk k1 p1 rib for 1$^1/_2$ in (4 cm), ending after a ws row.
Change to US size 10 (6 mm) needles.
Cont in st st until wrk meas 5$^1/_2$ [8:10$^1/_2$] in (14 [20:26] cm) from cast-on edge, ending with a ws row.

ARMHOLE SHAPING

Bind off 1 st at beg of next row, dec 1 st at same end of next, then ev alt row 1 [2:3] times. 14 [20:26] sts rem.
Cont in st st until wrk meas 11 [15$^1/_2$:20$^1/_2$] in (28 [40:52] cm) from cast-on edge, ending after a ws row.

SHOULDER SHAPING

Bind off 1 st at beg and at same end of ev row until 7 [10:13] sts rem.
Place rem sts on a stitch holder for front neck.

 CARDIGAN FRONT (RIGHT)

Work as left but reverse all shapings.

 SLEEVES (MAKE TWO)

Using US size 8 (5 mm) needles and col A, cast on 20 [28:36] sts.
Wrk k1 p1 rib for 1$^1/_2$ in (4 cm) in, ending after a ws row.
Change to US size 10 (6 mm) needles.
Continue in st st.

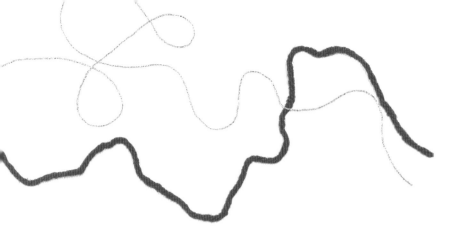

SLEEVE SHAPING

Inc 1 st at both ends of next and ev foll 3rd row 5 [8:9] times, then ev foll 2nd row 0 [1:4] times. 32 (48:64) sts rem. Cont without shaping until wrk meas 5$\frac{1}{2}$ [8:10$\frac{1}{2}$] in (14 [20:26] cm) from cast-on edge (or work to specific dog measurements), ending after a ws row. Bind off all sts.

 NECKBAND

Work with right side of all pieces facing. With col A and US size 8 (5 mm) needles, knit the sts held at right front, back neck, then left front neck. Wrk k1 p1 rib for 1$\frac{1}{2}$ in (4 cm), ending with a ws row. Next row, bind off all sts.

 HAT

Using US size 8 (5 mm) needles and col A, cast on 50 sts. Wrk k1 p1 rib for 2 in (5 cm), ending after a ws row. Next row, p all sts. Cont in st st following crown shaping.

CROWN SHAPING

K4, *k2tog*, rep from * to * to end. Next and ev alt row p all sts. K3, *k2tog*, rep from * to * to end. K2, *k2tog*, rep from * to * to end. K1, *k2tog*, rep from * to * to end. Draw the yarn through the last sts and pull together.

 **EPAULETTES (MAKE TWO)**

Using US size 8 (5 mm) needles and col A, cast on 7 sts. Wrk k1 p1 rib for 2 [2$\frac{1}{2}$:2$\frac{1}{2}$] in (5 [6:7] cm), ending after a ws row. Next row, *k1, inc 1, wrk to last st,

inc 1, wrk to end*. Next row, p all sts. Next row rep from * to *. Next row p all sts. Cont on k1 p1 rib until wrk meas 4 [4$\frac{1}{2}$:5$\frac{1}{2}$] in (10 [12:14] cm) from cast-on edge, ending after a rs row. K2tog, wrk to last 2 sts, k2tog. Bind off all sts.

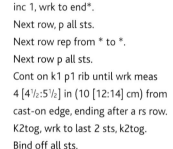

MAKING UP

🐾 JACKET

1 Pin the outside edges of the left and right front shoulders to the markers on the back armhole edges. Stitch in place.

2 Join the side seams and the sleeve seams.

3 Place a marker pin halfway along each front armhole. Then pin each sleeve seam to a marker, and stitch the sleeves into the armholes.

🐾 BRAIDING

⬆ **1** Hand stitch gold braid along the top of the ribbing around each sleeve cuff and around the lower edge of the jacket. Now stitch gold braid to both center front edges.

⬅ **2** Use pins to mark the positioning of five gold frog fasteners along the front opening. Make sure the fasteners are evenly spaced before stitching them securely in place.

 **EPAULETTES**

◄ 1 Using a US size 7 (4 mm) crochet hook and col B, work a crochet edge around the outside edge of each epaulette. Now work a second crochet row onto the first (see crochet diagram on page 31).

2 Work a tasseled trim around the wider part of the epaulette. Trim to 1¹⁄₂ in (4 cm).

▼ 3 Stitch each epaulette to the shoulders of the jacket.

 HAT

◄ 1 Join the crown and side band seam.

2 Hand stitch two bands of gold braid to the lower and upper edges of the ribbed side band on the hat.

3 Stitch a length of elastic to the hat as a chin strap, to keep it in place on the dog's head. Measure the dog first!

ESKiMo CHiC

CHILL OUT

Brrr... chilly day? Your pooch won't need to worry about the cold when he wears his furry hooded Eskimo suit. The body of the suit is made from a really chunky yarn so it's very quick to knit, and warm and snug for your dog to wear. For the perfect finishing touch, add a fluffy crochet edge and hood lining using a fabulous fur-effect yarn. You can use a toning shade, or even a vivid contrast color if your dog is feeling frivolous!

YOU WILL NEED

pair of US size 10$\frac{1}{2}$ (6.5–7.5 mm) needles

pair of US size 15 (10 mm) needles

pair of US size 6 (4 mm) needles

2 [5:8] x 3$\frac{1}{2}$ oz (50 g) balls of DK yarn
in color A (ivory)

3 [4:6] x 1$\frac{1}{2}$ oz (50 g) balls of DK fur-effect yarn
in color B (beige/brown)

stitch holder

tape measure

safety pins

US size 10$\frac{1}{2}$ (6.5–7.5 mm) circular needle

US size 6 (4 mm) crochet hook

bodkin

glass-headed pins

stiff card

scissors

KEY COLOR A—HEAVY WEIGHT YARN, IVORY
COLOR B—FUR-EFFECT YARN, BEIGE/BROWN

KNITTING UP

SPECIAL ABBREVIATIONS

(See page 11 for general abbreviations.)
Hooded vest is worked in k1 p1 rib throughout.

TENSION

9 sts and 12 rows measured over a 4 x 4 in (10 x 10 cm) square of stocking stitch worked on US size 15 (10 mm) needles.

Am I feeling frivolous enough for vivid contrast colors—or should I go for a subtle look?

BACK

Using US size 10½ (6.5–7.5 mm) needles and col A, cast on 26 [36:46] sts.
K 3 rows then wrk k1 p1 rib until wrk meas 1½ in (4 cm).
Change to US size 15 (10 mm) needles.
Cont in k1 p1 rib until wrk meas 5½ [8:10½] in (14 [20:26] cm) from cast-on edge.

ARMHOLE SHAPING
Bind off 1 [1:1] st at beg of next 2 rows, dec 1 st at both ends of next, then ev foll 0 [2:2] rows 0 [1:2] times.
22 [30:38] sts rem.
Cont until wrk meas 11 [16:20½] in (28 [40:52] cm) from cast-on edge, ending after a ws row.
Mark both ends of this row with safety pins or short lengths of yarn to indicate the beginning of the hood section.

Measure 2¾ [4:5] in (7 [10:13] cm) down each side from top of work.

Mark these two points with safety pins or short lengths of yarn to indicate how far to stitch the front shoulder along the back armhole edge.

HOOD

Cont working k1 p1 rib on remaining sts at back neck, until wrk meas 22 [29½:38½] in (55 [75:98] cm) from the cast-on edge.
Bind off all sts.

HOOD LINING
Using US size 6 (4 mm) needles and col B, cast on 78 [110:140] sts.
Cont in st st until wrk meas 22 [29½:38½] in (55 [75:98] cm) from cast-on edge.
Bind off all sts.

FRONT (LEFT)

Using US size 10½ (6.5–7.5 mm) needles and col A, cast on 9 [13:17] sts.
K 3 rows then wrk k1 p1 rib until wrk meas 1½ in (4 cm).

Change to US size 15 (10 mm) needles.
Cont in k1 p1 rib until wrk meas 5$\frac{1}{2}$
[8:10$\frac{1}{2}$] in (14 [20:26] cm) from
cast-on edge.

ARMHOLE SHAPING

Bind off 1 [1:1] st at beg of next row,
wrk to end, then dec 1 st at same end
of next then ev foll 0 [2:2] rows 0 [1:2]
times. 7 [10:13] sts rem.
Cont until wrk meas 11 [16: 20$\frac{1}{2}$] in
(28 [40:52] cm) from cast-on edge,
ending after a ws row.

SHOULDER SHAPING

Bind off 2 sts at beg of next row and
at same end of ev alt row 2 [3:4}
more times, then bind off rem 1
[2:3] sts.
Work right front in the same way
reversing all shapings.

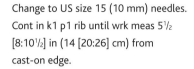 **NECKBAND**

Work with rs of all pieces facing.
Using a US size 10$\frac{1}{2}$ (6.5–7.5 mm)
circular needle and col A, pick up and
knit 52 [70:88] sts along the right front
edge up to the hood seam. Pick up the
same number of sts from the hood
seam down the left front edge.
Wrk k1 p1 rib for 4 rows, then k 3 rows.
Bind off.

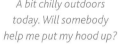 **ARMHOLE BANDS**

Pin the outer edge of each shoulder
seam to the marker on the back
armhole/shoulder edge. Join neckband
and shoulder seams.
Using US size 10$\frac{1}{2}$ (6.5–7.5 mm)
needles and col A, pick up 30 [40:50] sts
around the armhole edge.
K 3 rows then wrk k1 p1 rib for 3 rows.
Bind off.
Work other armhole band in same way.

*A bit chilly outdoors
today. Will somebody
help me put my hood up?*

MAKiNG UP

🐾 VEST

1 Join the side seams and armhole band.
2 Fold the hood section in half with right sides together. Join the hood seam.

🐾 FURRY EDGE

1 Using the crochet hook and col B, work three rows of single crochet around both armholes, the neck, hood, and hem edge.

🐾 HOOD

⬆ **1** Fold the hood lining in half with right sides together. Join the top seam.

⬅ **2** Place the hood lining inside the vest hood with wrong sides together. Pin the edge of the lining to the neckline of the garment and the outer edge of the ribbed hood band. Using col B, stitch the lining to the garment, taking care not to pull the stitches too tight.

 POM POMS

1 Cut two circles of card about 3 in (8 cm) in diameter, then cut a smaller hole about 1 in (2.5 cm) in diameter in the center of each. Place the two pieces together, then wind a length of col B through the center and around the outside of the circle.

◄ **2** When the center of the circle is full of yarn, snip the loops around the outside edge using small scissors.

⬆ **3** Pull the card circles apart a little then tie two strands of col B tightly around the center. Remove the card circles. Then make another pom pom in the same way.

◄ **4** Make two 12 in (30 cm) long crochet chains using col A (*see page 31*). Stitch one end to the garment and thread the other through a pom pom.

SUNFLoWER

FUN IN THE SUN

I challenge anyone to remain straight faced when they see this outfit—it never fails to raise a smile. Our model looks absolutely delighted to be a sunflower—just look at his great big grin! The sleeveless stripy vest and headband are worked in rib throughout so are comfortable and easy to wear. Don't worry, the petals are stiffened with very thick fluffy pipe cleaners so won't hurt your dog's face at all.

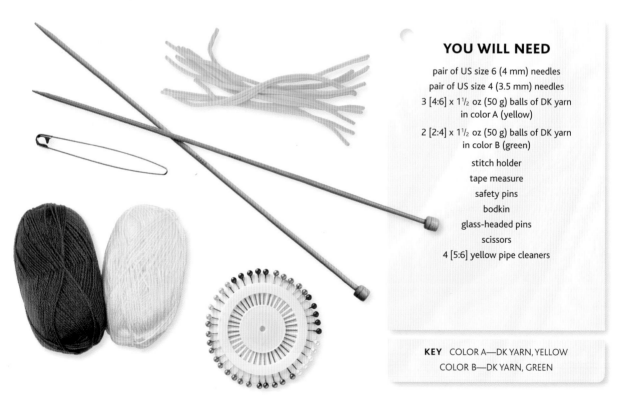

YOU WILL NEED

pair of US size 6 (4 mm) needles
pair of US size 4 (3.5 mm) needles
3 [4:6] x 1$\frac{1}{2}$ oz (50 g) balls of DK yarn
   in color A (yellow)
2 [2:4] x 1$\frac{1}{2}$ oz (50 g) balls of DK yarn
   in color B (green)

stitch holder
tape measure
safety pins
bodkin
glass-headed pins
scissors
4 [5:6] yellow pipe cleaners

KEY COLOR A—DK YARN, YELLOW
COLOR B—DK YARN, GREEN

KNiTTiNG UP

 SPECIAL ABBREVIATIONS
(See page 11 for general abbreviations.)
PATT—work 2 rows col A then 2 rows col B.
NOTE—vest worked in k1 p1 rib throughout.

 TENSION
22 sts and 30 rows measured over a 10 x 10 cm (4 x 4 in) square of stocking stitch worked on US size 6 (4 mm) needles.

 BACK
Using US size 4 (3.5 mm) needles and col A, cast on 60 [88:114] sts.
Wrk k1 p1 rib for 1 row.
Change to col B and wrk 2 rows.
Cont in patt and k1 p1 rib for 1 1/2 in (4 cm), ending after a ws row.
Change to US size 6 (4 mm) needles.
Cont in patt and k1 p1 rib until wrk meas 5 1/2 [8:10 1/2] in (14 [20:26] cm) from cast-on edge.

ARMHOLE SHAPING
Bind off 2 [2:3] sts at beg of next 2 rows, dec 1 st at both ends of next, then ev foll 3 [2:2] rows 1 [3:4] times. 52 [76:98] sts rem.
Cont until wrk meas 11 [16:20 1/2] in (28 [40:52] cm), from cast-on edge, ending after a ws row.

Place all stitches on stitch holder for back neck.
Measure 2 3/4 [4:5] in (7 [10:13] cm)

down each side from top of work. Mark these two points with safety pins or short lengths of yarn to indicate how far to stitch the front shoulder along the back armhole edge.

FRONT
Using US size 4 (3.5 mm) needles and col A, cast on 54 [78:100] sts.
Wrk k1 p1 rib for 1 row.
Change to col B and wrk 2 rows.
Cont in patt and k1 p1 rib for 1 1/2 in (4 cm), ending after a ws row.
Change to US size 6 (4 mm) needles.
Cont in patt until wrk meas 5 1/2 [8:10 1/2] in (14 [20:26] cm) from cast-on edge.

ARMHOLE SHAPING
Bind off 2 [2:3] sts at beg of next 2 rows, dec 1 st at both ends of next, then ev foll 3 [2:2] rows 1 [3:4] times. 46 [66:84] sts rem.
Cont in patt until wrk meas 11

[16:20 1/2] in (8 [40:52] cm) from cast-on edge, ending after a ws row.

SHOULDER SHAPING
Bind off 2 [2:2] sts at beg of next 12 [16:20] rows. 22 [34:44] sts rem.
Place remaining sts on stitch holder for front neck.

NECKBAND
NOTE—work with right side of all pieces facing.

Using US size 4 (3.5 mm) needles and col A, wrk all the stitches held at front and back neck in k1 p1 rib.
Cont in patt and k1 p1 rib until neckband measures 3 [4:4 3/4] in (8 [10:12] cm).
Next row bind off all sts.

ARMHOLE BANDS
Pin the outer edge of each shoulder seam to the marker on the back

armhole/shoulder edge. Join neckband and shoulder seams.

Using US size 4 (3.5 mm) needles and col A, pick up 60 [90:114] sts around the armhole edge.

Wrk 1 row k1 p1 rib.

Change to col B, wrk 2 rows k1 p1 rib.

Change to col A, wrk 2 rows k1 p1 rib then bind off all sts.

Work the other band in the same way.

🐾 PETAL HEADBAND

PETALS

Using US size 4 (3.5 mm) needles and col A, cast on 3 [3:3] sts.

1st and ev alt row p all sts.

2nd row, k1, inc 1, k1, inc 1, k1 = 5 sts.

4th row, k2, inc 1, k1, inc 1, k2 = 7 sts.

6th row, k3, inc 1, k1, inc 1, k3 = 9 sts.

8th row, k4, inc 1, k1, inc 1, k4 = 11 sts.

10th row, k5, inc 1, k1, inc 1, k5 = 13 sts.

12th row, k6, inc 1, k1, inc 1, k6 = 15 sts.

14th row, k7, inc 1, k1, inc 1, k7 = 17 sts.

16th row, k8, inc 1, k1, inc 1, k8 = 19 sts.

18th row, k9, inc 1, k1, inc 1, k9 = 21 sts.

Cont in st st until wrk meas 3 [4:4¾] in (8 [10:12] cm) from cast-on edge.

Place on stitch holder.

Make 8 [10:12] petals in total.

HEADBAND

Transfer all the sts on the stitch holder to a US size 4 (3.5 mm) needle, making sure that the right side of all the petals is facing. 168 [210:252] sts in total.

Using US size 4 (3.5 mm) needles and col A, wrk the next row as follows:

k2tog 5 times, k1, k2tog 5 times, rep from * to * 7 [9:11] times more. 88 [110:132] sts rem.

Next row *p2tog, p7, p2tog*, rep from * to * 7 [9:11] times more. 72 [90:108] sts rem.

Cont in k1 p1 rib as follows:

Wrk 2 rows col A, 2 rows col B, 2 rows col A, 2 rows col B, 2 rows col A.

Next row, bind off 36 [45:54] sts using col A, break off the yarn and leave rem sts on needle.

On the other needle cast on 36 [45:54] sts in col B, then work the sts left on the needle.

Next row wrk all sts in col B.

Rejoin col A and cont in patt for 14 rows.

Next row, bind off all sts.

MAKING UP

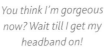

You think I'm gorgeous now? Wait till I get my headband on!

VEST

1 Join side seams and armhole bands.

HEADBAND

1 Join the short ends of the ribbed band together to make a cylinder (or leave this till the end). You will see that the cast-off/cast-on row leaves a slot for the dog's ears!

2 Cut each pipe cleaner in half.

3 Bend the ends of the pipe cleaner sections into small loops, twisting to secure them so that there are no sharp edges to hurt the dog.

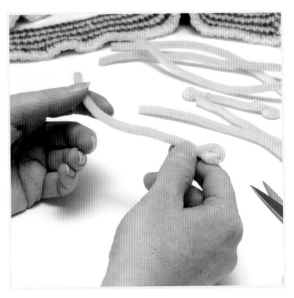

◄ **4** Attach a short length of col A to the wrong side of a petal close to the base. Use two or three small stitches to secure one looped end of a pipe cleaner to the base of the petal.

↑ **5** Now secure the pipe cleaner to the center of the petal using a loose stitch resembling a zigzag.

◄ **6** When you reach the top of the pipe cleaner, secure the looped end to the petal as before. Attach a pipe cleaner section to the other petals in the same way.

PREPPY SWEATER

STUDIOUSLY STYLISH

A real American classic, this slouchy sweater looks a little like a baseball jacket with a two-tone design and stripy ribbing. Our preppy sweater has a knitted shield on the back bearing a monogram—just to give it a personal touch! You can work the shield motif into the garment piece using the Intarsia method, or knit it separately and then stitch it on by hand when the garment is complete.

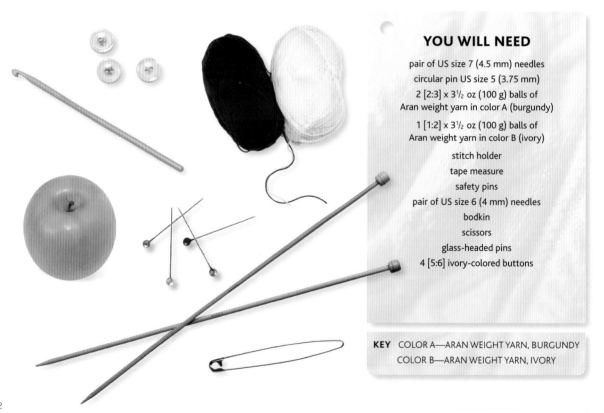

YOU WILL NEED

pair of US size 7 (4.5 mm) needles

circular pin US size 5 (3.75 mm)

2 [2:3] x 3$\frac{1}{2}$ oz (100 g) balls of
Aran weight yarn in color A (burgundy)

1 [1:2] x 3$\frac{1}{2}$ oz (100 g) balls of
Aran weight yarn in color B (ivory)

stitch holder

tape measure

safety pins

pair of US size 6 (4 mm) needles

bodkin

scissors

glass-headed pins

4 [5:6] ivory-colored buttons

KEY COLOR A—ARAN WEIGHT YARN, BURGUNDY
COLOR B—ARAN WEIGHT YARN, IVORY

KNiTTiNG UP

🐾 SPECIAL ABBREVIATIONS

(See page 11 for general abbreviations.)

🐾 TENSION

19 sts and 24 rows measured over a 4 x 4 in (10 x 10 cm)
square of stocking stitch, worked on US size 7 (4.5 mm)
needles.

🐾 BACK

Using US size 5 (3.75 mm) needles
and col A, cast on 54 [76:98] sts.
Cont in k1 p1 rib, wrk 1 row.
Change to col B, wrk 4 rows.
Change to col A, wrk 2 rows.
Change to col B, wrk 4 rows.
Change to US size 7 (4.5 mm)
needles and col A.
Cont in st st until wrk meas 5¹/₂
[8:10¹/₂] in (14 [20:26] cm) from
cast-on edge.

ARMHOLE SHAPING

Bind off 2 [2:2] sts at beg of next 2
rows, dec 1 st at both ends of next
and ev alt row 0 [1:2] times. 48 [68:88]
sts remain.
Cont in st st without shaping until
wrk meas 11 [16:20 ¹/₂] in (28 [40:52]
cm) from cast-on edge, ending after
a ws row.

Place all stitches on stitch holder for
back neck.
Measure 2³/₄ [4:5] in (7 [10:13] cm)
down each side edge from top of work.
Mark these two points with safety pins
or short lengths of yarn to indicate how
far to stitch the front shoulder along
the back armhole edge.

LEFT FRONT

Using US size 5 (3.75 mm) needles and
col A, cast on 19 [28:37] sts.
Cont in k1 p1 rib, wrk 1 row.
Change to col B, wrk 4 rows.
Change to col A, wrk 2 rows.

Change to col B, wrk 4 rows.
Change to US size 7 (4.5 mm) needles
and col A.
Cont in st st without shaping until wrk
meas 5¹/₂ [8:10¹/₂] in (14 [20:26] cm)
from cast-on edge, ending with a ws
row.

ARMHOLE SHAPING

Bind off 2 [2:2] sts at beg of next row,
dec 1 st at same end of next and ev alt
row 0 [1:2] times. 16 [24:32] sts rem.
Cont in st st without shaping until wrk
meas 7 [10:13] in (17.5 [25:32.5] cm)
from cast-on edge, ending after a
ws row.

NECKLINE SHAPING

With rs facing, dec 1 st at end of next
row, and at same end of next and ev 3
[4:3] rows 3 [8:15] times, then ev 4 [4:0]
rows 3 [2:0] times. 9 [13:16] sts rem.
Cont without shaping until wrk meas
11 [16:20¹/₂] in (28 [40:52] cm) from
cast-on edge.

SHOULDER SHAPING

With rs facing, bind off 3 [3:2] sts at beg of next row, then bind off 2 [2:2] sts at same end of ev alt row 3 [5:7] times. Snip off yarn and draw it through the last st to complete.

🐾 RIGHT FRONT

Work as left front, reversing all shapings.

🐾 SLEEVE (MAKE TWO)

Using US size 5 (3.75 mm) needles and col B, cast on 24 [34:44] sts.
Cont in k1 p1 rib, wrk 1 row.
Change to col A, wrk 4 rows.
Change to col B, wrk 2 rows.
Change to col A, wrk 4 rows.
Change to US size 7 (4.5 mm) needles and col B.

SLEEVE SHAPING

Cont in st st and inc 1 st at both ends of next and ev 3 [3:3] rows 7 [11:15] times.
You will now have 40 [58:76] sts.
Cont without shaping until wrk meas 8 [10^{1}/$_{2}$:12^{3}/$_{4}$] in (20 [26:32] cm) from cast-on edge (or work to specific dog measurements), ending after a ws row.
Bind off all sts.

NECKBAND

Work with right side of all pieces facing.

Using a US size 5 (3.75 mm) circular pin and col B, pick up and knit 70 [100:130] sts from lower right center front, working up to the shoulder. Knit all sts held at back neck, then pick up and knit 70 [100:130] sts from left shoulder seam to the lower center front edge.
Change to col A, wrk 3 rows in k1 p1 rib.
Change to col B, cont in k1 p1 rib, wrk 2 rows.
Change to col A, wrk buttonhole row.
Wrk 4 sts *k2tog (or yo), wrk 10 sts*. Rep from * to * 3 [4:5] more times. Cont in rib to end.
Wrk 3 more rows in col A.
Change to col B, wrk 2 rows.
Next row, bind off all sts.

I'll be the smartest dog in the library today!

MAKING UP

🐾 JACKET

1 Pin the outside edges of the left and right front shoulders to the markers on the back armhole edges. Stitch in place.

2 Join the side seams and sleeve seams.

3 Place a marker pin halfway along each front armhole. Pin the sleeve seams to the markers, then stitch the sleeves into the armholes.

➡ **4** Stitch the buttons to the button band to correspond with the buttonholes.

🐾 KNITTED SHIELD

1 Using size 6 (4.5 mm) needles and col B, cast on 12 st.

2 Continue working from the chart opposite in col A and col B together, using the Intarsia technique (*see pages 16–17*). Each light square on the chart represents one stitch col B and each dark square one stitch col A.

SHAPING

Inc 1 st at both ends of foll 13 rows until you have 38 sts. Cont without shaping until the chart is complete then bind off all sts.
NOTE On a rs row, follow the chart from right to left.
On a ws row, follow the chart from left to right.

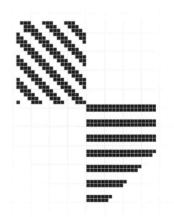

ABCDEFG HIJKLM NOPQRS TUVWX YZ

WORKING THE LETTER

1 Take care to center the design carefully. Choose a letter of the alphabet. Find the center point on the chart below, then mark it with a pencil.

2 Now, find the center of the upper left-hand portion of the shield and mark with a pin.

3 Count the squares downward and outward from the center on the chart to locate the lower right-hand corner.

Do likewise on the shield to establish your starting point.

4 You may now work the letter onto the knitted shield using the Swiss embroidery technique (*see page 17*) using col A.

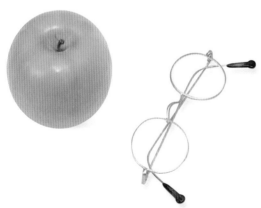

SHIELD MOTIF

1 Pin the shield motif centrally to the back of the jacket.

2 Stitch the shield to the jacket, then slipstitch neatly around the edge.

GiDDY UP!

LEAD THE WAY

Make sure your doggy is first past the post when racing around the park—don't forget to adjust the chinstrap so he doesn't lose his hat in the process! The jockey shirt and hat are knitted in stocking stitch throughout using vibrant colors to resemble racing silks. Practice the Intarsia technique when using more than one color yarn in a row, just to make sure there are no holes in your knitted pieces!

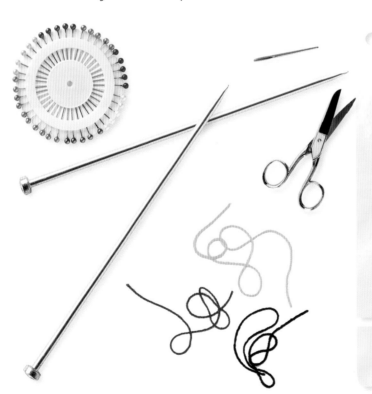

YOU WILL NEED

pair of US size 4 (3.5 mm) needles

pair of US size 6 (4 mm) needles

1 [2:3] x 1½ oz (50 g) ball of DK yarn in color A (royal blue)

2 [3:4] x 1½ oz (50 g) balls of DK yarn in color B (yellow)

1 [2:3] x 1½ oz (50 g) ball of DK yarn in color C (black)

stitch holder

tape measure

safety pins

glass-headed pins

scissors

bodkin

20 in (5 cm) of ¼ in (5 mm) wide black elastic

KEY COLOR A—DK YARN, ROYAL BLUE

COLOR B—DK YARN, YELLOW

COLOR C—DK YARN, BLACK

KNiTTiNG UP

🐾 SPECIAL ABBREVIATIONS
(See page 11 for general abbreviations.)

🐾 TENSION
22 sts and 30 rows measured over a 4 x 4 in (10 x 10 cm) square of stocking stitch, worked on US size 6 (4 mm) needles.

🐾 BACK
Using US size 4 (3.5 mm) needles and col A, cast on 62 [88:114] sts.
Wrk k1 p1 rib for 1$\frac{1}{2}$ in (4 cm), ending after a ws row.
Change to US size 6 (4 mm) needles.
Next row, wrk 31 [44:57] sts in col A, then wrk rem sts in col B using the Intarsia method.
Cont in st st until wrk measures 5$\frac{1}{2}$ [8:10$\frac{1}{2}$] in (14 [20:26] cm), from cast-on edge.
Next row, work 31 [44:57] sts in col C, then wrk rem sts in col A. P 1 row.

ARMHOLE SHAPING
Bind off 2 [2:3] sts at beg of next 2 rows, dec 1 st at both ends of next, then ev foll 3 [2:2] rows 1 [3:4] times. 54 [76:98] sts rem.
Cont without shaping until wrk meas 11 [15$\frac{1}{2}$:20$\frac{1}{2}$] in (28 [40:52] cm) from cast-on edge, ending after a ws row.

Place all stitches on stitch holder for back neck.
Measure 2$\frac{1}{2}$ [4:5] in (7 [10:13] cm) down each side from top of work. Mark each of these two points with safety pins or short lengths of yarn to indicate how far to stitch the front shoulders along back armhole edges.

🐾 FRONT
Using US size 4 (3.5 mm) needles and col A, cast on 54 [78:98] sts.
Wrk k1 p1 rib for 1$\frac{1}{2}$ in (4 cm), ending after a ws row.
Change to US size 6 (4 mm) needles.
Next row, wrk 27 [39:49] sts in col A, then wrk rem sts in col B using the Intarsia method.
Cont in st st until wrk meas 5$\frac{1}{2}$ [8:10$\frac{1}{2}$] in (14 [20:26] cm) from cast-on edge.
Next row work 31 [44:57] sts in col C, then wrk rem sts in col A. P 1 row.

ARMHOLE SHAPING
Bind off 2 [2:3] sts at beg of next 2 rows, dec 1 st at both ends of next, then ev foll 3 [2:2] rows 1 [3:4] times. 46 [66:82] sts rem.
Cont without shaping until wrk meas 11 [15$\frac{1}{2}$:20$\frac{1}{2}$] in (28 [40:52] cm) from cast-on edge, ending after a ws row.

SHOULDER SHAPING

Bind off 2 [2:2] sts at beg of next 12 [16:20] rows. 22 [34:42] sts rem. Place all stitches on stitch holder for front neck.

 ## SLEEVE (LEFT)

Using US size 4 (3.5 mm) needles and col C, cast on 30 (45:60) sts. Wrk k1 p1 rib for $1\frac{1}{2}$ in (4 cm), ending after a ws row. Change to US size 6 (4 mm) needles and cont in st st, following pattern thus: wrk 8 rows col A, 8 rows col C.

SLEEVE SHAPING

Inc 1 st at both ends of this and then of ev foll 3 [3:3] rows, 10 [16:18] times, 52 [79:98] sts rem. Cont without shaping until wrk meas 8 [$10\frac{1}{2}$:$12\frac{1}{2}$] in (20 [26:32] cm), from cast-on edge (or to specific dog measurements), ending after a ws row. Bind off all sts.

 ## SLEEVE (RIGHT)

Follow same instructions but use col B throughout.

NECKBAND

Work with right side of all pieces facing. Using US size 4 (3.5 mm) needles and col C, pick up and knit the stitches held at front and back neck. Wrk k1 p1 rib for $1\frac{1}{2}$ in (4 cm), ending with a ws row. Next row, bind off all sts.

 ## HAT

Using US size 4 (3.5 mm) needles and col C, cast on 20 sts. Cont in k1 p1 rib, wrk 1 row. Next row wrk 1 st, inc 1 st, wrk to last st, inc 1 st. Rep last row twice more. You will now have 26 sts. Break off yarn and place sts on stitch holder. Next row cast on 26 sts, wrk sts from stitch holder, then use another length of yarn in col C to cast on a further 26 sts. You will now have 78 sts. Wrk k1 p1 rib for 1 in (2.5 cm), ending after a ws row. Change to US size 6 (4 mm) needles and cont in st st until wrk meas 4 in (10 cm) from cast-on edge, ending after a ws row. Follow pattern thus: wrk 4 rows col B, 4 rows col A, 4 rows col B, 4 rows col C.

CROWN SHAPING

1st row, *k2tog, k4*, rep from * to * to end. 65 sts rem. Next and ev alt row, p all sts. 3rd row, *k2tog, k3*, rep from * to * to end. 52 sts rem. 5th row, *k2tog, k2*, rep from * to * to end. 39 sts rem. 7th row, *k2tog, k1*, rep from * to * to end. 26 sts rem. 9th row, k1, *k2tog, k1*, rep from * to * to last st, k1. 14 sts rem. Snip off the yarn and draw it through the remaining sts to pull them together.

MAKING UP

🐾 SHIRT

1 Join the neckband.

2 Pin the outside edges of the left and right front shoulders to the markers on the back armhole edges. Stitch the shoulders in place.

3 Join the side seams and sleeve seams.

4 Place a marker pin halfway along each front armhole. Then pin the sleeve seams to the markers, and stitch the sleeves into the armholes.

Galloping geldings! Do you think I can carry off a hat as well?

STAR MOTIF

1 First locate the center of the yellow colored sleeve both vertically and horizontally. Then mark this position with a pin.

2 Now refer to the star motif chart (below) and mark the center in both directions again using a pencil.

3 Count the squares of the motif downward and across to the right to reach the lower right-hand point of the star. Count the rows and stitches from the center marker pins on the sleeve to establish the same point.

4 You may now begin to work the motif using the Swiss embroidery technique using col A. Then work the star motif on the upper left quadrant on the garment front in the same way.

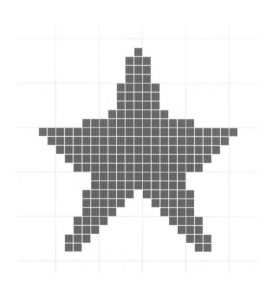

 HAT

1 Thread the tail at the top of the hat onto a bodkin, then use it to join the crown seam.
◄ ↓ **2** The ribbed hatband and brim are a little floppy and may fall over the dog's eyes! In order that the brim stays in a cute turned up position, simply slip stitch the top of the brim to the crown of the hat as shown.

◄ **3** Stitch a length of elastic to the hat as a chin strap, to keep it on the dog's head. Measure the dog first!

FROGGY FASHION

JUMP TO IT

Ribbitt, ribbitt! Doggy or froggy? Our Jack Russell terrier was the perfect choice for this outfit—he could hardly resist jumping from lily pad to lily pad! We used a smooth, silky yarn and rib (ribbitt!) stitch throughout, so this outfit is stretchy, smooth and close fitting. No decent frog outfit would be complete without a pair of bulging froggy eyes! These are filled with polyester wadding so they are very lightweight for the froggy doggy to wear.

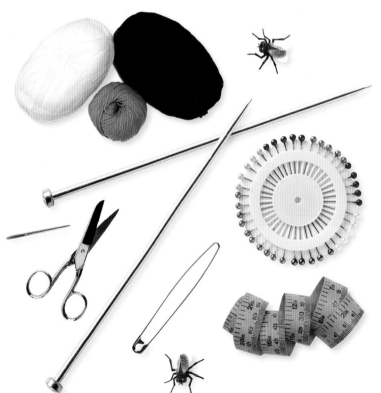

YOU WILL NEED

pair of US size 6 (4 mm) needles

pair of size 10 (6 mm) needles

5 [6:8] x 1½ oz (50 g) balls of medium-weight yarn in color A (green)

1 x 1½ oz (50 g) ball of medium-weight yarn in color B (white)

1 x 1½ oz (50 g) ball of medium-weight yarn in color C (black)

stitch holder

tape measure

safety pins

bodkin

scissors

glass-headed pins

small amount of polyester wadding to stuff eyeballs

KEY COLOR A—GREEN, COLOR B—WHITE
COLOR C—BLACK

KNiTTiNG UP

 SPECIAL ABBREVIATIONS

(See page 11 for general abbreviations.)

Garment is knitted entirely in k1 p1 rib.

 TENSION

15 sts and 22 rows measured over a 4 x 4 in (10 x 10 cm) square of stocking stitch, worked on US size 10 (6 mm) needles.

 BACK

Using US size 6 (4 mm) needles and col A, cast on 42 [60:78] sts.

Wrk k1 p1 rib for 1^1/$_2$ in (4 cm), ending after a ws row.

Change to US size 10 (6 mm) needles.

Cont in k1 p1 rib until wrk meas 5^1/$_2$ [8:10^1/$_2$] in (14 [20:26] cm) from cast-on edge.

ARMHOLE SHAPING

Bind off 1 [1:1] st at beg of next 2 [2:2] rows, dec 1 st at both ends of next, then ev foll 2 [3:4] rows 1 [2:3] times. 36 [52:68] sts rem.

Cont until wrk meas 11 [16:20^1/$_2$] in (28 [40:52] cm) from cast-on edge, ending after a ws row.

Place all stitches on stitch holder for back neck.

Measure 2^3/$_4$ [4:5] in (7 [10:13] cm) down each side from top of work.

Mark these two points with safety pins to indicate how far to stitch the front shoulder along the back armhole edge.

 FRONT

Using US size 6 (4 mm) needles and col A, cast on 36 [52:68] sts.

Wrk k1 p1 rib for 1^1/$_2$ in (4 cm), ending after a ws row.

Change to US size 10 (6 mm) needles.

Cont in k1 p1 rib until wrk meas 5^1/$_2$ [8:10^1/$_2$] in (14 [20:26] cm) from cast-on edge.

ARMHOLE SHAPING

Bind off 1 [1:1] st at beg of next 2 [2:2] rows, dec 1 st at both ends of next, then ev foll 2 [3:4] rows 1 [2:3] times. 30 [44:58] sts rem.

Cont until wrk meas 11 [16:20^1/$_2$] in (28 [40:52] cm) from cast-on edge, ending after a ws row.

SHOULDER SHAPING

Bind off 2 [2:2] sts at beg of next 8 [12:16] rows.

Place rem 16 [20:26] sts on stitch holder for front neck.

 SLEEVES (MAKE TWO)

Using US size 6 (4 mm) needles and col A, cast on 21 [30:39] sts.

Wrk k1 p1 rib for 1^1/$_2$ in (4 cm), ending after a ws row.

Change to US size 10 (6 mm) needles.

SLEEVE SHAPING

Inc 1 st at both ends of next, then of ev foll 5 [5:5] rows 6 [10:13] times.

Cont without shaping until wrk meas 8 [10$\frac{1}{2}$:12$\frac{3}{4}$] in (20 [26:32] cm) from cast-on edge (or work to specific dog measurements), ending after a ws row. Bind off all sts.

🐾 HEADBAND

Using US size 6 (4 mm) needles and col A, cast on 50 [66:80] sts.
Wrk k1 p1 rib for 3 [4:4$\frac{3}{4}$] in (8 [10:12] cm).
Next row, bind off first 25 [33:40] sts, break off the yarn and leave rem sts on needle.
On the other needle cast on 36 [45:54] sts in col A, then work the sts left on the needle.
Next row wrk all sts.
Cont in k1 p1 rib for another 2$\frac{1}{2}$ in (6 cm).
Next row, bind off all sts.

EYE

Using US size 10 (6 mm) needles and col A, cast on 15 sts then p 1 row.
Next row, k1, *inc 1, k1*, rep from * to end. 29 sts.
Cont in st st until wrk meas 3 in (8 cm) from cast-on edge, ending with a ws row.
Change to col B, wrk 3 rows.
Next row, k2, *k2tog, k3*, rep from * to * to last 2 sts, k2. 24 sts.

Change to col C, then wrk 1 row.
Next row, *k2tog, k2*, rep from * to *. 18 sts.
Wrk 1 row.
Next row, *k2tog, k1*, rep from * to * to end. 12 sts
Wrk 1 row then rep last row. 8 sts.
Break off the yarn, thread it onto a bodkin then pass it through all sts, drawing up tightly.

NECKBAND

Work with rs of all pieces facing.

Using US size 6 (4 mm) needles and col C, pick up and knit the sts held at front and back neck.
Wrk k1 p1 rib for 1$\frac{1}{2}$ in (4 cm), ending with a ws row.
Next row, bind off all sts.

*Give me a kiss then!
I might turn into a
handsome prince!*

MAKiNG UP

TOP

1 Join the neckband.

2 Pin the outside edges of the left and right front shoulders to the markers on the back armhole edges. Stitch the shoulders in place.

3 Join the side seams and sleeve seams.

4 Place a marker pin halfway along each front armhole. Then pin the sleeve seams to the markers, and stitch the sleeves into the armholes.

HEADBAND

↑ 1 Secure the end of the thread that draws up the black "pupil" at the center to prevent unraveling, then join the eyeball seam.

← 2 Flatten the eyeballs, positioning the seam in the center of the under side. Make a small fold in the green part of the upper side so that the folded edge meets the edge of the pupil as shown. Stitch the fold in place.

⬑ **3** Fill the eyeballs lightly with polyester stuffing. Run a short length of yarn through the cast-on edge and draw up tightly. Secure the yarn to prevent the stuffing escaping from the eyeballs.

⬆ **4** Place the eyeballs onto the narrow section of the headband and stitch in place as shown.

⬑ **5** Join the short ends of the ribbed band to make a cylinder. You will see that the cast-off/cast-on row has resulted in a slot for the dog's ears!

INDEX